Hand in Hand

Connecting One Hand at a Time

Janice Hale-Harris

Library of Congress Control Number: Pending

ISBN: Softcover: 978-0-9855479-0-5

ISBN: EBook 978-0-9855479-2-9

Copyright 2012 HIH Publishing

First Printing 2012

To order additional copies of this book, contact:

CreateSpace

www.createspace.com

Cover Design by NYCE Graphics

Houston, Texas

For the two people who first touched

me and held my hand,

Beulah and James,

my mom and dad.

"Touch is one of the wonderful gifts we are given, but most of us have forgotten how to use this powerful skill to help increase the quality of our lives...."

Rainer Maria Rilke

Madison, Ava and Dee got off the school bus near Madison's home. All three girls were quiet which was uncommon for the normally chatty crew. Earlier that day they found out their friend Kayla was moving away. It had always been the four of them and they could not imagine life without Kayla. The girls sat on the front porch at Madison's house, shoulders slumped, still not saying a word. Madison's dad pulled into the driveway. When he saw the girls he immediately knew something was wrong.

"Well hello there. Why such long faces?" he asked. They each looked up at him but no one responded. It looked like each girl was on the verge of breaking into tears if a word was spoken.

Finally Madison blurted out "Kayla is moving away and we don't want her to go."

"Well," Madison's dad said, "this will change things for all of you a bit, but remember you will still be able to call and text each other. You can probably even visit from time to time." The three preteens looked up at him with a 'yes we already know that look'. Madison's dad just shook his head and walked into the house.

Later that evening Madison was sitting at her computer getting ready to start her homework. "What are you so down in the dumps about?" KJ asked.

"Go away." Madison said.

"Whatever," KJ replied. "I'm just trying to be brotherly."

Madison had a big project for her world cultures class. The teacher allowed them to choose groups of up to four people for the project. Of course, Madison, Ava, Dee, and Kayla were a natural fit. Now Kayla was leaving and there was no one else to add to their group. That actually was fine because the girls did not want another partner. They just wanted Kayla to stay. The teacher told the class to create a project about something they could do or invent that would make a difference in the world around them. Some of the groups were doing projects on the environment. Others chose recycling. Some groups were working on songs they thought would move the world. Madison and her friends were drawing a blank on project ideas because they seemed to focus only on Kayla's leaving. It was Friday evening and the girls were getting together the next day. Madison decided to tackle the project issue tomorrow.

Madison woke up Saturday morning to the smell of French toast cooking in the kitchen. That meant one thing, her grandmother, Nana Rose was there. Nana Rose would always make breakfast for Madison and KJ when their dad and Papa went on early-morning fishing trips. Nana would come over and make herself at home, cooking, cleaning and dabbling until Dad and Papa returned with their catch of the day. Nana Rose was always a bright spot for Madison, especially since her mom died of cancer a few years ago. Madison pulled herself out of bed and went downstairs.

"Good morning Sunshine Madison" Nana Rose said as she gave Madison a big hug. "How's my favorite granddaughter this morning?"

"I'm good," Madison sighed with her elbows on the counter and her hands under her chin.

"Hmm, that good doesn't sound so good to me." Nana Rose said.

At that moment, KJ walked into the kitchen, overhearing what his grandmother had just said.

"Are you still balling because your little foursome is breaking up? Get a life already, it's not like she's going away forever," KJ taunted his sister.

"Who's moving away?" Nana Rose asked.

Madison gave her brother the evil eye and then turned to her grandmother. "Kayla is moving because her mom got a new job. Her mom wanted to try to keep her in school here until the end of the school year, but that's not working out, so Kayla has to move. We are working on a group project for our world cultures class. All the other groups have four people and now we only have three members. And we're all so upset about Kayla leaving we can't come up with a project idea."

"Well," Nana Rose said, "This does seem like a dilemma. What is the subject for the project?"

Madison sighed again. "We have to come up with an idea that will make our world better. We can't seem to think of anything another group hasn't already chosen. The project is in two weeks so we are going to get together this afternoon and try to come up with an idea."

"When is Kayla moving away?" Nana Rose asked.

"She leaves at the end of the month."

"Well, Sunshine Madison, I think I might have an idea that can help you with your project and cheer you girls up about Kayla moving away. Are the girls coming over here later?"

"Yes ma'am, they are."

"Well then, I will still be here and I can tell you all about a possible idea. Would that be alright with you and your friends?"

"Oh yes Nana Rose. My friends always love coming over when you're here" Madison exclaimed.

15

"Well then, let's eat breakfast so you and KJ can clean the kitchen. Then, I'll cook something special for your group meeting." Nana Rose smiled at Madison.

"If Nana Rose is cooking for your friends, then I'm inviting some of the fellas over to watch the game so we can grub too!" KJ smirked.

"Nana Rose, tell him NO BOYS!" Madison said in a loud voice.

Nana Rose just laughed and said, "KJ you must first ask me if I am up to cooking enough food to also feed your friends. It's not polite to assume."

"Sorry Nana Rose. Can my friends come over too?" KJ asked in a pleading voice tinged with a smile.

"Of course, but you and your friends will have to watch TV in the game room downstairs and not disturb the girls while they are working. Is that a deal?"

"Sure we don't want to be around them anyway," KJ laughed. "You know how much all the guys love it when you cook for us."

Then Nana Rose turned to Madison. "Sunshine, be sure to invite Kayla to come over with the other girls. Even though she can't be a part of the project, I think she will enjoy hearing my idea," Nana Rose said to Madison.

"I'll text everybody now Nana Rose. Thanks." Madison said.

Not only did the kids love Nana Rose's cooking, they loved hearing her sing as she cooked. Most of all they loved her stories. Nana Rose could make simple things seem less complicated. Hurts didn't seem so deep and disappointment always seemed to have a good and right ending, once she finished explaining another way to see the situation. She was everyone's favorite Nana, young and old alike.

This was going to be a banner food day. A great breakfast, a Nana Rose lunch, and a fish fry with the day's fresh catch when Papa Tom and Dad came home. For a moment, Madison's mind left

the sadness of Kayla's leaving to relish all the good smells that
would be around her.

The doorbell rang and Madison ran to let her friends inside.
To her dismay, it was Mike and Ethan, KJ's irritating friends.
Madison just looked at them and didn't speak. She gave them her
best, 'I don't really like you look' which only made them laugh. KJ
appeared at the door and took his friends into the kitchen to say hello
to Nana Rose. Once all the hellos were done, the boys headed for
the game room with cold drinks in hand. The next sound of the
doorbell had to be Madison's friends. Dee's mom dropped the girls
off at Madison's house. Ava's dad was going to pick them up later.

That afternoon, the house was full of young folks, just the
way Nana Rose liked things. Dad and Papa had returned from
fishing. They were in the backyard cleaning their catch. The house
was in full motion.

"Nana Rose says she has an idea we might want to use for
our project," Madison told her friends."

"Well I hope it's a good one because we are running out of time," Ava said.

Kayla sat quietly not saying much. She was very sad about leaving her friends and felt she was letting them down with the project. Just then, Nana Rose appeared in the family room with a tray of sandwiches and paper plates for the girls.

"I thought I would let you all get your food first," Nana Rose said. You know the boys don't believe any food should be left for anyone else when they start eating." The girls laughed and chose their sandwiches.

Nana Rose said, "I'll be right back. I'm going to put the rest of the sandwiches in the kitchen and tell the boys the food is ready."

A few minutes later, Nana Rose returned to the family room. She sat down with the girls and smoothed out her top. "Well, ladies you know how much I love to share my stories with you. When Madison told me about your project and Kayla moving away, I thought to myself, I know just the remedy for your project and four broken hearts. Are you ready to hear all about it?" The girls nodded in unison. Their minds drifted towards thoughts of Kayla

leaving. They were beginning to feel too choked up to speak.

Nana Rose began. "Several years ago, I had a friend who

moved away. Evelyn was my best friend in the world. Her mom

and my mom were best friends. The summer between sixth and

seventh grade, Evelyn's mom was killed in a terrible car accident.

Her sister Cheryl was hurt and spent a long time in the hospital.

Everyday my mom and dad would go to the hospital to see Evelyn's

sister Cheryl. Everyday Cheryl asked when was her mom coming to

see her. It was so sad. Weeks later, Evelyn's sister was released

from the hospital and a few months later, Evelyn's dad decided to

move. He said there were too many memories in the house for him

to keep living there. I couldn't believe Evelyn wasn't going to be

right down the street. Every time I thought about her moving I

would start to cry. My mom saw me in one of my sad moments and

asked me if I would like a way to stay connected to Evelyn even

though she was moving away. Well, I said yes. Staying in touch

back then wasn't as easy as it is today. We only had one phone line in the house for the entire family to use. We didn't have cell phones or email or tweeter."

"It's Twitter, Nana Rose" Madison laughed. The other girls laughed too.

"Yes, well, we didn't have that either" Nana Rose said. "Anyway, where was I? Oh yes, my mom said she had an idea about how we could stay connected. My mom told me there was a Bible verse about people touching and agreeing about concerns, cares for others, and questions that did not seem to have an answer. The verse said 'where two or more are gathered…', but none of that made sense to me at the time. Then my mom asked me could I think of a way to always feel in touch with Evelyn even if we didn't talk on the phone or write letters? I could not think of anything. She told me to find the verse in the Bible and read it each night, sleep on it and the answer would come. A few days later, right before Evelyn's move, I got the perfect idea. I grabbed my notebook and ran down to Evelyn's house the next day. I asked her to trace her hand in my book. She gave me a very strange look and asked me why. Then, I told her about the Bible verse and said whenever you are sad or worried I will lay my hand in your hand and pray for you and send you good thoughts. Evelyn was so touched by the thought of this she started to cry. Then, she went and got her notebook and I traced my hand in her book.

You see, girls, your hands have healing energy that's available when you share your traced hand with each other. I had Madison and KJ trace their hands for me when they were much younger. They thought it was just a fun summer project. But for me, whenever I sense something might be bothering them and they need a soothing touch, I just get out their handprints."

Madison sat there in awe. She remembered tracing her hand when she was about five years old, but she thought her grandmother was just giving her a fun project to do. Now she felt even more loved knowing what Nana Rose had been doing for her and KJ for years.

"What would happen if the people around the world shared a healing touch with others?" Nana Rose asked. "There's been a lot of research done on the healing power of touch. What if you girls did some research on touch for your project and started your own Hand Books with each other? Now, this is just an idea from an old grandma, but I don't think anyone else in your class will have this thought. Why don't you girls marinate on the idea for a while and see what you think. I'm going to check on the boys and then I'm going to the backyard to see what's taking so long with the fish cleaning."

The girls sat there for a moment before anyone spoke. They wondered if this idea would work. Where would they find more information about the healing power of touch?

Then Kayla spoke in a soft voice. "I want to trace my hand and give a drawing to each one of you. Then I would still be part of the project even if I'm not here. Even if you don't do the project, I like the idea of staying in touch this way. It seems so, so, I don't know….warm and caring."

The other girls sat there thinking about the idea. Thoughts started flowing.

Ava was the first to speak. "This idea is fresh and it could be a symbol for a world movement. People connecting with other people through touch. Maybe we should write down some research ideas we could use for our project."

Madison said, "I'll get some paper and take notes."

The girls were quiet but their brains were turning in many directions. A Hand Book….a Hand Book.

Madison returned with the paper. The first thing they did was pass sheets of paper around and each girl traced her hand on three different pieces of paper. Once they completed this task, each girl took one of each other's handprints. Now each had a set of three handprints from their friends. They sat there looking at the handprints feeling inspired that they were on to something big and powerful. What was the next step? The research.

Ava spoke first. "Let's look on the Internet and see what we can find out about the power of touch. Maybe we can find some cool information to support our handbook."

Madison said, "I'll compile a list of things from the Internet and then we can divide up the information we find to get started on our project."

The other girls nodded in agreement.

Then, Kayla spoke up. "Even though I won't be here, I want to have my hand included in the book and maybe I can come up with a title for the project and the handbook. Is that okay with you guys?

"

"Sure," they all said in unison.

"Okay," Madison said, "I'm going to get my laptop and we can start finding topics we can research."

The more information the girls found about the power of touch, the more excited they became. By the time Ava's dad got there to pick up the girls, they were back to their old, familiar chatty selves. Ideas were flowing. Their energy was high. Even the boys darting in and out of the room didn't faze them. All the girls felt they were on to something big. Each person had her assignment and all systems were go on the project.

Then, Kayla said, "Wait, we have to do one more thing." She grabbed a few pieces of paper and went into the kitchen.

"Nana Rose," she said. "Would you trace your hand for us to include in our books?"

Nana Rose smiled. "Of course, I will. That is so sweet of you all to want to include me."

Nana Rose traced her hand four times and gave a sheet to each of the girls. The girls were excited and their project was taking shape. They only had two weeks to pull everything together, but this didn't feel like a project anymore. The assignment felt more like a calling and a gift to share with others. Maybe this is why their teacher created the assignment in the first place. Their project would make a difference in the lives of others and hopefully the world.

The research was coming along well. For the next weeks, Madison, Ava and Dee worked on their project pieces in every spare moment. The following Friday after school, the girls felt themselves falling back into a slump. Kayla was leaving the next day. This was going to be their last night together. They decided to have a slumber party at Madison's house. Kayla's mom thought that would be a great idea.

When Madison's dad arrived home from work, he called out Madison and KJ's names. They were in their separate rooms and each felt a little worried from the sound of their dad's voice. Madison and KJ came downstairs. Their dad was sitting at the kitchen table. They looked at their dad, but neither of them said a word. Their dad finally spoke. "Nana Rose was having shortness of breath this afternoon, so Papa Tom took her to the doctor. The doctor admitted her to the hospital for some tests, but we are going to trust and pray she will be just fine. Nana Rose said not to worry. And Madison, she wanted me to tell you to just stay focused on your project. I know the girls are planning to come over this evening. Nana Rose wants you to keep your plans and not worry. I can take you and KJ to the hospital tomorrow to see Nana Rose."

Madison tried not to worry, but she couldn't help herself. Her friends were on their way over and everyone would be sad to hear about Nana Rose. The doorbell rang and the girls were there.

Once they were inside, Madison told them about Nana Rose being in the hospital. They all sat there for about 30 minutes saying nothing.

Then Kayla spoke up. "Maybe we should connect with Nana Rose using our Hand Books. I made four different covers for us and we just have to put our pages in the book."

Kayla took out the covers she made and the girls were amazed at how beautiful the covers were. Kayla had named the project Hand In Hand, Touching and Connecting One Hand at a Time. The girls loved the title. It conveyed everything they wanted to say. Then without even speaking, they each pulled out their page with Nana Rose's handprint and placed their hand in her hand. Minutes went by. One by one, they seemed to start feeling better. They each felt a real connection to Nana Rose and to each other.

Madison finally spoke. "Kayla, the book covers are beautiful and I love the name. I think it's a great name for our project."

The other girls nodded in agreement.

Just then KJ came into the room. "What are y'all doing?" he asked.

"Go away." Madison said to him.

But, Kayla spoke up and told him, "We're putting our hand in Nana Rose's hand so we can feel her energy."

"That's stupid." He said, but he had a curious look on his face.

Kayla went on. "Nana Rose told us about connecting with one of her friends that moved away when she was a girl and this is something we are doing for our project. We traced our hands and asked Nana Rose to trace her hand, so we could feel connected to her and each other at any time."

Madison added, "Yeah, Nana Rose has been connecting to me and you since we were little through our hand prints."

KJ stood there for a moment remembering tracing his hand a long time ago. Then he asked Madison if he could see her book. Madison handed the book to KJ and he turned to the page with Nana Rose's handprint. KJ gently placed his hand in Nana Rose's hand. Even though he didn't want to admit it to the girls, he felt comforted using the handbook.

KJ turned to them and said, "I gotta give it to you. This is pretty cool." He slowly left the room.

Even though this was supposed to be an evening of fun, the girls could not help working on the project and talking about their research. This had become an outpouring of passion to give a gift to the world.

The next morning the girls left early. Madison, KJ and their dad were about to leave the house to visit Nana Rose at the hospital when the phone rang. The caller ID showed Papa's number. They all froze. Dad picked up the phone and had a brief conversation with Papa Tom.

When he hung up, he turned to Madison and KJ and said, "Well there's no need to head to the hospital." Madison and KJ were barely breathing. "Nana Rose is on her way home."

They all broke into smiles with high five's and hugs all around.

"Papa Tom said she should rest today and we can come over tomorrow to spend time with them" Dad said with a joyful voice.

Madison and KJ went back to their rooms. A few minutes later, KJ came to Madison's room. "Hey Madison, do you think Nana Rose could really feel your energy through the handbook thing you guys are doing?" KJ asked.

"I think so." Madison replied. "We've been doing a lot of research for our project and we're excited about the possibilities."

"What kind of possibilities?"

"Can I read you part of our report?" Madison asked.

"Sure." KJ said.

"Well, we learned that energy never really goes away. Sometimes it just changes forms, like H^2O can be water, or ice, or snow, or sleet, but it is still H^2O. We found out that babies who are sick or abandoned recover better and have fewer problems when they are gently touched regularly. There's a group of foster-type grandparents who go to the hospital just to hold sick babies. We found other websites that talked about the same thing for elderly people. We even found a study that shows basketball teams where the players touch each other with high fives, shoulder jabs, and even pats on the back have higher winning percentages than players who hardly ever touch each other. We learned in other countries, people tend to touch each other more than we do in America, and they seem to have more personal connections than we do. Some people are doing research to show that people spend so much time on the computer, texting or tweeting that we have new connections to people, but we don't develop as many deep relationships. They believe physical touch has reduced in ways which have affected all types of relationships, even marriages. So, through our project, we are giving people a new way to have real connections to the person or people whose handprints are in their personal Hand Book. Just like Nana Rose has been doing with us all these years."

"Wow, that's pretty cool." KJ said which was quite a compliment coming from him.

The following week, the girls presented their project to the class. The girls demonstrated how the Hand Book works.

Madison spoke for the group. "First, you ask someone you care about to trace their hand on a piece of paper. Then, when you feel a need to connect to that person, you simply lay your hand on their handprint. You, then, can pray for that person, think good thoughts about him or her, and feel connected to their energy."

Everyone was so moved by the story of Nana Rose and her friend, the research they presented and how they used the book when Nana Rose was in the hospital, the entire class wanted to make Hand Books for their families and friends.

Their project went viral. Classmates emailed, tweeted and texted their friends and began collecting each other's handprints.

The stories were amazing. One classmate had a brother in the military. He asked his brother to trace his hand and mail it to him. He told the class it was the highlight of his week when he received the traced handprint in the mail. He felt he could connect with his brother anytime he wanted by just laying his hand in his brother's handprint.

Another classmate's mom taught elementary school. She had her entire class make Hand Books for each other. Her students' parents loved the idea.

KJ found the article online about the basketball team that won more games when they touched each other. His teammates created a Hand Book with all the team members' handprints. They would all lay their hands on the book just before the game started to connect with each teammate.

The girls' teacher, Ms. Moore had a relative going in the hospital. She asked her cousin to trace her hand in Ms. Moore's handbook so she could pray for her while Ms. Moore was on break during the school day.

Madison, Ava and Dee found themselves keeping in touch with Kayla to help make book covers for other people. Because of Nana Rose, the four friends had accomplished a goal even bigger than their assignment. They decided to create a special Hand Book for Nana Rose, so they could reach out and touch her anytime they needed encouragement or just the touch of their best mentor. When the girls gave the book to Nana Rose she could not hold back her tears. She was so proud of everything they had accomplished. They had found a way to give a gift to the world to encourage others to stay in touch, literally. The friends felt blessed beyond measure to have their alliance with each other, their families, (especially Nana Rose), and a real connection to each other.

Hand In Hand, we can connect to others and heal our world, one touch at a time.

Add your Hand to the Movement.

###

Steps to Creating a Hand In Hand Journal

1. Purchase a Hand In Hand Journal at

   http://thehandinhandbook.com

2. On the first page write your intentions for the people who will put their handprints in your journal.

   Example: I am so grateful to share the gift of prayer with the people whose handprints are in my journal. Thank you for the opportunity to connect to them one hand at a time.

   Example: This journal is my prayer vehicle for those I love and care for. Thank you for the gift of touching them whenever the need arises.

   Example: God is my source and I am the conduit. I am so blessed to have the honor of linking with you through this hand journal. Thank you for trusting me to pray and connect with you.

3. Ask each person to put their hand on one page in the book. (it does not matter if it is their right or left hand)

Ask them to trace their hand, sign their name and include the date.

4. On the back of the page of each person's handprint feel free to record anything you wish about answered requests concerning this person.

5. Share your amazing stories at

http://www.thehandinhandbook.com

Handy Resources

Hand Books and journals for gifts:

http://www.thehandinhandbook.com

Sharing your stories: http://www.thehandinhandbook.com/

Connect with me online: janice@thehandinhandbook.com

Like us on Facebook: http://facebook.com/thehandinhandbook

Tweet us at: http://twitter.com/handinhand2012

My Hand Holders

There are many people to thank for holding my hand on this journey. Friends from so many parts of my life have been my greatest encouragers: Debra King, Nedaro Bellamy, Demetrice Tillman, Evelyn Turner, Ellen Junious, Kelly Stallings, Mary Underwood, Jay Whitsett, Sandra Woods, Linda Marks, Debbie Eldridge, Jorge and Pat Quinones.

Thank you to my young readers, Chloe Hinton, Mia Harris, Kayla Tillman, and Ainsley Johnson. My Spiritual Director teachers, (Glendyn Bode, Connie Bovier, and Becky Oates) were the catalyst for this project. Thank you for your commitment to walk beside me, encouraging my spiritual journey.

A special thanks to my publishing family; Rita Mills and Terry Bessard. This book would not have been possible without your guidance and wisdom.

My son Kenan and my daughter Kori, who held my hand tightly, reviewed, edited, challenged and loved me through the entire journey. You are truly the greatest gifts God could have ever given me. Yours are the first hands in my Hand Book.

Moreover, special thanks to all my readers for taking this journey and giving love to others in a very special way. Thank you for embracing the Hand Book project and sharing your energy with others. Our world is better because you are here.

About the Author

Janice Hale-Harris is originally from Buffalo, NY. She attended Syracuse University and received a BS degree in Broadcast Journalism. She holds an MBA from Texas Woman's University and she is a certified International Spiritual Director. During the past decade, Janice has been connecting to others through her personal Hand Book. Currently she lives and works in Houston, Texas.